What It Might Mean

Victor Klimoski

2011

Createspace • Amazon.com Company

Cover: From the Antelope Canyon Series
John Gorton (Staples, Minnesota)

Back Cover: Michael Dennis Browne, *What the Poem Wants: Prose on Poetry* (Carnegie Mellon University Press, 2009). Used with author's permission.

Printed in the USA by createspace.com
ISBN-13: 978-1466467323
ISBN-10: 1466467320

Copyright © 2011 Victor Klimoski * All rights reserved.

Contents

Paying Attention

Call to Attentiveness/6
Inscription/7
Choosing A Path/8
Full Consent/9
Invocation At Dawn/10
Meditation/11
Revelation/12
Jubilate/13
Slow of Heart/14
Truth In Advertising/15
Human Culpability/16
A Lesson About Death/17
The Way Forward/18
Vespers/19
Compline I/20
Compline II/21

Sending Down

Penitent/24
A Lesson on Prayer/25
Introibo Ad Altare Dei/26
Old Time Religion/27
Baltimore Catechism/29
Gathering the Scattered/30
The Imperfect Teacher/31
Oration/32
Where I Belong/33

Taking In

Bewilderment/36
On the Seventh Day/37
Voice in the Wilderness/38
Annunciation/39
Incarnation/40
Starlight/41
Lenten Bell/42
Stone Sober/43
Homespun Remedy/44
Shipshape/45
Gathered from the Storm/46
Splitting Hairs/47

Looking Far

Nearsighted Theory/50
Knowledge of God/51
What A Friend We Have/52
Keeping the Record Straight/53
Ponderable Images/54
Kept God/55
What the Apple Knows/56
Sunday Preacher/57
Brother Andre/58
Lost Recipe/59
A New Age/60
Think Again/61
Searching for a Future/62
All Souls Day/63
Unbreakable Bond/64
Communion of Saints/65

Paying Attention
*What captures our attention, teaches.
And it is often the most ordinary
occurrence that teaches best.*

The Call To Attentiveness

For each day to be grand
requires a faint blue-glimmered sunrise
combusting hot in a flash
and quickening the shades of night.

There must be a body of water,
A lake or river chanting softly.
Throw in a flock of cardinals for descant
And leaves lisping a simple psalm.

Bank the path with fresh bloomed clover.
Let the strawberries be overripe
so they fall at the slightest touch,
their delicate smell lingering for hours.

Let the day unfold gradually,
Attentive to each passing minute.
Be alert as silky grass ripples,
drawing you into fields wide as lakes.

Follow as your shadow dances
across the span of the day and arrives
home weary, ready to sleep,
your hair smelling of spice and sea air.

Inscription

Across the pale blue sky
A small black bird flies,
Its name lost as it signs
The page of a new day.

The light is frail and pure,
Neither the bright glare of noon
Nor the slight scowl of dusk
As cows silently file home.

This light is breath, word
Spoken in an unknown tongue
And rising on the wind
As everything stirs from sleep.

For now we read the message
A small black bird writes in cursive,
Always hopeful we will discover
What lies behind the text.

Choosing A Path

Eyes wearied by night watch,
Squint as the sun rises.
The path along the shore,
bending toward the water,
extends far beyond safe, dry ground.

Sunrises like this cast a spell.
Stones become lava, gulls speak in oracles.
Even the thin blue sky shatters,
Its fracture lines revealing
How delicate creation can be.

My burning eyes cannot turn aside
From this brilliant revelation.
All my fears fall like scales,
And I wonder where I would end
    if I stepped even now
        on the slowly fading path.

Full Consent

Embrace this day.
Make no long range plan
Or list of duties.
Stand here -
        unmoving.
Watch closely this garden.
Learn what you can
When you finally,
        willingly,
    say yes.

Invocation At Dawn

Put a spirit of fervor in me,
Something white hot
To fire a heart nearly blue
               with cold.

Let me believe wide-eyed
In forgotten promises
I long ago bound with cord
And left in the attic like a set
of National Geographics.
Release my mind for fantasy,
Visions so colorful,
               so bold
I nearly stop breathing.

Remove my scorn for hope,
My envy of those who keep dreaming
Despite the evidence.

Open the door just a crack
               so light may enter,
making even a scratched floor
worthy of a waltz.

Meditation

Early on,
we learn to work.
We make things,
dig holes,
pound nails,
pull weeds,
clean the house.

Still,
sitting here
as the sun rises,
    just sitting
as waves roll up
on the stony ledge,
virtue is set free
from pinched anxiety
about proving one's worth.
Greeting the sun
is important work,
a responsorial hymn
so profound
I may not be able to move
                all day.

Revelation

We know the way, the signposts,
All the travel guides written
In elegant script with bright pictures.
If a stranger asks, we describe
Where to turn, which routes to avoid,
Shortcuts that will save time.
We cross the distance in our mind's eye,
Sure of our way, our compass true.

We are nearly always surprised
When we end up in a cul de sac
Or discover a pile landslide of stones
Where we swear was once a crossroads.
We find ourselves walking in circles,
Doubling back when the ground softens
Or we can't recall a lightning-split cedar
Lying in despair along the trail.

Sometimes we need to force ourselves
To stand still in one spot,
To spread our maps upon the ground
To study them closely, use the legend.
And when we look skyward
For the angle of the sun or the North Star,
We set out as for the first time,
More modest in our certainty,
       more attuned to natural signs.

Jubilate

Any psalm more eloquent
Than this flawless lake
Must have a line
Able to stop conversation.
Its metaphors, woven from gold,
Will need to catch the sun,
Changing ordinary light to fire,
Setting ablaze the trees.
It must be free of anger,
Boasts of destruction or threat.
Instead it needs to sigh,
Barely perceptible
But loud enough
To silence even the birds.

Slow of Heart

Just when I think
I've turned a new leaf,
left behind bad habits
and wasteful distractions,
I suddenly veer across the median,
right in the path of a ten-ton truck.

The impact throws me for a loop.
I stagger from the ditch
seeing stars in midday light,
swearing I never saw it coming
or heard the horn
or saw the flash of the silver grill
smiling carnivorously
at one more sap
asleep at the wheel
and dreaming of soft landings.

Truth In Advertising

The path is not easy
Despite what you've heard.
The sight from high summits
Comes after endless climbing
And wading fetid swamps
And crossing deep ravines
Dense with thorns and fanged snakes.
Is it strange so many
Turn back at the first bend,
Content with a snapshot
Taken from an airplane?

Human Culpability

Failure tempers arrogance,
The delusion we've escaped
Handicaps and impediments
The rest of humanity suffers.
The belief we are the burnished star
In a mediocre sky
Deflates in the face of sloth,
Lust, greed, avarice, envy,
Pride, hardness of heart –
The catalogue of our DNA.

What small comfort there is
Is knowing, though darkly,
How our soft underside
Does not exile us from the Garden.
For the invitation exceeds merit
Or efforts to prove our worth.
And that alone should humble us
On days everything works
And we swear we've reached
                perfection.

A Lesson About Death

Only the foolish imagine
Death as a surprise,
As though it sneaks in,
Hides behind the curtain,
Waiting for the right moment
To lower the boom.

When asked, the ancients said
To live each day
As though it were the last,
The end a way to measure
What's worth the worry,
What's just a waste of time.

The admonition comes to me
As I'm prodded and poked
By someone assessing my flesh,
Looking serious and intent.
It leaves me wondering what's next
Now that all the surprise is gone.

The Way Forward

It is not complex,
though not for the timid,
for those seeking six steps
to perfection, the secret of life
wrapped in delicate gauze
It's as simple as giving away
your second coat,
half the pantry,
the time you horde and count
like a bag of rare gold coins.
It is as soft as forgiveness
and as monumental as sitting
next to the woman you knew
from across the room
would be annoying.

Vespers

Let no one lose heart
As nightfall comes sailing
On waves across the lake.
Let the night birds rise,
The mists beneath them,
Billowy banks of water
Obscuring the shore.
Let stars appear in the millions,
Scattered like diamonds,
A few pictures taking shape,
Their stories so old we recall
How temporary we actually are.

Compline I

Give us light when dark
Is nailed against day's end.
A thin shaft is all we need
To guide our weary feet.
Let a beam as fine as dust
Lead us safely
Through the night
To the other side
Where morning opens wide.

Compline II

On dark nights when bats dart
Across a violet sky,
Don't go in until you've sung
A psalm to the setting sun.

Reach down and run your hand
Across the dampening grass.
Breathe in until your lungs ache,
Exhaling into the cool night air.

Now you are ready for bed
Once you've named the day's blessings,
Like the cardinal that flew by at dawn,
His feathers on fire in the sunlight.

Sending Down

Where we put down roots impacts deeply the values that last. Their durability and influence can surprise us for a lifetime.

Penitent

My father was a stub of a man,
short and thick, broad muscled back
with beefy hands so calloused
he seldom needed gloves
      when he worked his forge.

With one of those same hands,
he'd end his monthly confession,
striking his breast saying,
"My Jesus, mercy, Jesus mercy,
      my Jesus mercy."

He was not a foolish man,
prone to pious or vain speech,
"My Jesus mercy" came
from deep within his soul
      where dwelt his trust in God.

His contrition gave him courage
when he failed, when sin won,
when he felt his heart split
under the sharp blade of truth.
      Then the new priest came to town,

Found my father's contrition odd,
not the form listed in the book.
From behind the grill came the word,
a penance all nearby could hear,
      to learn by rote the proper words.

So at sixty-five my father,
his heartfelt sorrow found wanting,
learned someone else's words,
said them rightly though when done
      touched his breast as his amen.

A Lesson On Prayer

There wasn't a day she didn't pray,
that form of speech a natural dialect
mastered over a lifetime.
She prayed as she breathed:
without it she could not live.

Her piety was neither feigned
                    nor unctuous
except in church where her voice
went up an octave
as though God required singsong
to carry petitions above the rafters.

She wore her prayer with flawless ease,
a shawl woven of ancient thread.
She taught us the same by word
                    and deed,
preparing us for a journey
for which one tongue alone
                    would never do.

Introibo Ad Altare Dei

My childhood church is a knotty pine box
built on a hill high above the river,
above my house and the two-room school
where I learned that what lasts
is not built by human hands.

My childhood church bears the sweat
of my father's hands, my mother's brow
as he with hammer and saw,
she with skillet and pan
built the pews and fed the crowds.

In my childhood church we knelt
in our pew with our mother,
her sing-song voice one pace behind,
while my father's rich baritone
added timber to the choir.

In my childhood church the miracle
was the building, the gathering
at tables for meals, the stories
told to bind together families
across time and distrance.

If sacrament is a sign,
then the church on the hill
was our ark of covenant with God
who seemed content with knotty pine
and our efforts to live as one.

Old Time Religion

Like echoes from a deep canyon,
the old hymns come back.
Sometimes a chorus,
sometimes the first line
or just a phrase:
salve regina,
tantum ergo,
veni creator spiritus.
Not always Latin
though that dead tongue
still sings well,
carrying memories
wrapped tightly
against the elements.

At May evening devotions,
the priest in damasked cloak
calls out a litany,
his back bent over his book.
The servers twitch
trying to find a soft spot
for their knees.
The monstrance sparkles,
candelabra blaze as the litany
moves back and forth –
Mother of God, pray for us,
Mother of Heaven,
pray for us.
Pray for us.

The routine is dull, not boring.
The dead earnest voice of my mother
bites off the last few letters
of each acclamation.
And the hymns rise up,
ride on the Wurlitzer's tremolo
gaining momentum as voices
lock together
as do their lives.

Then it is over.
Coffee and cake in the hall.
Someone pulls out a deck of cards.
Stories begin,
and the hymns
reach a new level of harmony.

Baltimore Catechism

At seven I learned
my soul was white as milk.
Its angelic sheen would last
until my sins
    like bits of tar
began to dull its purity,
white bleeding to gray
then total obliteration.

At five I believed in angels,
elves and generous fairies.
By seven I learned
the terrible truth
that my slightest fault
could earn the wrath of God
and spoil forever
the taste of milk.

Gathering the Scattered

Someone finds a brown clay bowl,
its red lip chipped from mornings
when mother set flour and yeast.
The bowl is raised for all to see
and seeing they smell winter's first light.

Another declares, "Letters from Frank,"
an uncle lost in Vietnam lamenting
the foibles of generals and kings,
then asking if his dog, Judd,
would remember how he looked.

Aged clothes, faded photos, ticket stubs.
an empty earthen jug
smelling faintly of summer wine.
Postcards from France,
Fool's gold from the Black Hills.

In a box of kettles we find
a tattered cookbook
frail as parchment
written in five hands,
secret ways with common food.

This familial catacomb
opened by curiosity
illuminates what's been lost,
too common to be named heirloom,
too precious to be ignored.

The Imperfect Teacher

My father taught me little –
Not how to fish, hold a bat,
Fix the brakes,
Talk to women.
When men tell me
What they learned from their fathers,
I feel the pinch of regret,
The loss of what seems birthright.

My father taught me little,
Neither manual arts
Or how human beings relate
Though he did about steadfastness,
How a person's word
should mean something,
How belief in God rings dull
Without living proof in kindness.

My father taught me in his own way,
With lessons I might someday grasp
When I was ready to be instructed,
When my resistance to him softened
And my need for his perfection faded.

Oration

When my mother prayed aloud,
her voice rose and fell
like a little boat in a stream.
The lilt was annoying
to me at thirteen
afraid someone would note
her odd enunciation.

As distance of her absence grows,
I recall as sweet the cadence,
her prayers said with such sure belief
they'd reach a distant shore
and there cast anchor
for any fear she bore.

Where I Belong

The church is half-full,
Mostly families with claims
Barely thirty-years old,
Not like my own whose name
Has passed the century mark.
My visits are infrequent
But still I see familiar faces,
Know the color of their front doors,
What desserts at potlucks are theirs.

I close my eyes and hear
Voices of my mother and her friends
Drilling the rosary with industrial vigor.
I smell their perfumes and watch
Their mouths tight with holy chore.
I hear my father's voice rise in song,
His depth balancing the high notes
The women pile on the scale.

They've re-gilded the statues,
But their same faces shine through.
I take for granted the life size crucifix,
A full grown man nailed to it.
It was there from my birth,
Something I took for granted but sensed
It marked us for life.

Afterwards I am kissed and greeted,
An aging son of dead parents,
A boy still, returned for Mass,
And quickly found to be one of them.

Taking In
What we might end up believing is not sanitized doctrine, but the way the original story shapes and is shaped by our own.

Bewilderment

Out of gloom and darkness,
out of the sour mud of earth,
came the first signs of life.
No one can bear witness
whether beauty lay
beneath the dark slime.
We can only speculate
that the first mighty gasp for air
let loose a sound that echoes still,
the cry of bewilderment
in the face of such grand promise.

On the Seventh Day

Day by day the account
cleaves darkness from light,
gives order to chaos,
and stirs the earth madly
to loose its fermentation
in cascades of color and sound.

When humans appear,
most work's been done
except for naming
and for telling aloud
what should not be lost.
        for want of words.

Voice in the Wilderness

Intent from the start,
he studied all the parts
under a stern paternal eye.
He observed the rites, said the prayers
and one day slipped out of town
with walking stick
        and no change of clothes.

What happened next no one knows,
years re-forming him inside out,
emptying the chambers of his heart
for visions even he feared.

When he returned to the world,
his squareness was at odds
with its roundness and its love
of simple, clever answers.

He was a fright to see,
a nest for hair, a buckskin shift,
feet hard as stone.
Thin as a reed, his voice thundered
yielding no compromise.
People listened, then squirmed.
Some turned his way, most not.
Many hoped he would just find
        regular work.

Annunciation

I carry what sustains me
in pockets, brown paper bags,
backpacks strapped and zipped.
A book of poems, a working pen,
a postcard from Donegal,
photographs of those I love,
a set of psalms, a small pad of paper
so whenever the grace of a word
falls upon me like Gabriel's greeting,
I might hold it gently,
trusting its beauty will last
for a time much later
when light starts to fail.

Discourse On Incarnation

When we stray from equation to pulse,
to the nearly ungraspable assertion
that in some odd lapse of judgment
God took on flesh and breathed in
the very ethers of creation,
we cross our hands in self-protection.

Blood and breath mean body,
mean muscle and sweat, teeth and spit.
If body then touch, flesh to flesh,
the feel of bone beneath the skin,
the sensation of being recognized,
cold proof yielding to fleshly embrace.

By Starlight

It is the season of light,
cold nights lit by moonglow
and the slim glimmer of stars
dancing like fireflies in crystallized air.

It is the season of light
the bright flame of a candle
set in the window as beacon
to weary travelers lost in a storm.

It is the season of light
when sight regained sees new
the ordinary forms of daily life
as work of divine magnitude.

It is the season of light
when fright of darkness
finds its freedom in the steady beam
of a single star telling a single tale.

Lenten Bell

There will be one bell
    tolling softly,
like a nun welcoming us
into the cloister,
    the stillness
sombered by the season.

But the season is not for mourning,
though sorrow keeps its chair.
Nor is it raw visions of God
writhing in human pain,
    brutalized,
  left to die.

This season calls us apart,
if only in the small space
human hearts need,
from fruitless worry
over what cannot be undone.

It is a time of slowed pulses,
breaths taken deep into the belly,
and the unwinding of muscles
too long tensed against foes
whose power begins to wane.

The tolling of the Lenten bell
becomes a mother's voice
calling at the end of the day
for children running with the wind
and needing, for safety's sake,
    to come home.

Stone Sober: John 11, 43-45

Bound snug in strips of cloth,
his cold corpse ready to collapse,
Lazarus slept in his final fate.
His last thoughts jumbled fears
for deeds done and undone.

What began as muffled sound
slowly gained coherence,
forming the cadence of his name,
something he could not resist
even in his mournful wrappings.

Wrestled from death by his name,
He walked clumsily toward the voice,
his face shielded from the light,
not knowing whether it was day
or why the air smelled so fresh.

Homespun Remedy

He pinched a bit of earth,
then spit to make mud
and spread it over eyes
dead to shape or color.
Not oil from rare seeds,
no secret herbal salve,
but spit-made mud
smeared lavishly
over eyes buried alive.
As the potion worked,
the blind man saw
through slitted eyes
ribbons of light
spreading wildly like fire
set loose in dry grass.

Shipshape

The wind rises sharply,
Will not be docile
Or curb its headstrong ways.
On the open sea its muscle
Whips the water into a froth.

Foolish boatmen scramble,
Tie down the sail,
Lean hard on the rudder
Bailing water pouring in
Faster than they can empty.

But there he lies upon the nets,
His head nestled in his arm,
His chest rising, falling, gently.
They rouse him for safety's sake
So death not catch him by surprise.

He looks up, yawns, scratches
His beard, a puzzled look in his eyes.
He sees their panic, turns to the wind,
His words snatched and cast overboard
Before they hear what was said.

The wind, caught off-guard,
Collapses, falls into the water.
It sinks below the surface
In a frenzy of bubbles, its defeat
Lost in its slow, garbled drowning.

They are now speechless with awe
as he stretches and arches his back,
His eye neither on them or the water
But on the thin red line of light
Rising just above the distant shore.

Gathered From the Storm

In the locked room,
curtained windows
hold in the darkness
while outside the wind
swallows the house whole,
each timber, each board
straining against the force.
When lightning strikes,
it explodes into tiny fractals
settling on each head
like flames of a candle.
Though it lasts only seconds,
it is long enough to corrupt fear,
sending them into the street
babbling to anyone they met
as the world shifted on its axis.

Splitting Hairs

For centuries great minds
puzzled how three
could inhabit a single being,
like some freak
in a circus sideshow.

While scholars argued,
wars raged and the poor
scratched the earth
for what grew
among rocks and thistles.

It is not wasteful to ponder
how mysteries come to be
unless curiosity distracts us,
and theories crowd out
urgent claims for attention.

Looking Far
Sometimes standing too close obscures judgment. Distance offers another perspective, less distinct but far more provocative.

A Nearsighted Theory of God

If there is a God, such power
exceeds glib explanation,
a borrowed vocabulary.

Efforts to nail God to a wall
like the head of a prized antelope
end up in disappointment.

Ancients, stirred by the idea of God,
found their text on the horizon
under the depthless dome of sky.

For they knew in a near-sighted way,
the clearest signs would be found
in what was not close at hand.

In joy or sorrow, life or death,
human hearts divine mystery
under vast star-painted skies.

So read the guidebooks as you will
knowing their limits to tell it full.
Then step outdoors, look far.

Knowledge of God

The knowledge of God is thin
For the nature of the divine
Exceeds our imagination.
Rather, we hold scraps of paper
With ancestral stories written
In pencil, some lines erased.

We stand in a cloud of unknowing.
Like disciples on Tabor.
It takes all our courage
To rely on word of mouth, on those
Who saw something though obscured,
Who drawing close were overpowered.

That is the one fact we can hold:
Witness born across time.
We stew over it, resist it, take it apart
And still long to know as certain
The voice behind the veil,
Churning the dark deep water.

What A Friend We Have

We talk about Jesus
as though he were a neighbor,
someone we've known all our lives.
Like Mabel's son Earl,
born with one ear,
never quite able quite to fit in.
With scraps of stories
Several times removed
we create an account we argue
reflects inside knowledge,
though at best it's a product
of long memory and
        deep desire.

Keeping the Record Straight

So sure of God, we write
With a broad nib and indelible ink
so the bloated words add heft
to arguments pale and wan.

The only problem with our claims
Are their insistent boast
We've figured out the narrow gate,
how to wedge through a fat camel's ass.

Much of our text is best guess,
distilled from faint trace of mystery,
from rushing into a dense, thick cloud
and coming out reduced nearly,
        but not enough,
                to silence.

Ponderable Images

We treat the divine image
like crystal, tinsel thin
and unsettled by loud noise
    or stiff hands.

Speak softly lest you disturb
God's delicate state of mind
with tales of ominous signs
    or unseemly deeds.

Use words that boost morale.
God likes cheerfulness,
beaming smiles pasted on
    when he's in the room.

Kept God

We prefer God boxed,
sometimes in bronze or gold,
ornately scrolled
to signal royal presence.
We keep those boxes
in rooms half-lit,
where shadows form
like wings of angels.

Other boxes more plain
Have tight lids, sturdy locks
lest they suffer divine seepage.
Sometimes we might peek,
just a crack, just enough
to catch a sweet beatific aroma.
But mostly these boxes sit
within easy reach
when we need to make a point
or smack a cockroach
scurrying across the floor.

What the Apple Knows

Our kind,
so cocksure
we've eaten the apple
        undetected,
presume our right
to rule life, death
as though they're commodities
   up for grabs
on an open market.
When we reach out
expecting to find gold
and draw back a handful of ash,
we gasp,
then suddenly cover
       our shame.

Sunday Preacher

Fine bits of spit trail his words.
He tears through tons of rock
for the one pure vein of gold
able to fill their pockets.

His shoulders twitch
from fear he's not been clear,
that his fervent exclamations
sound like drunken babble.

He works up a sweat,
Smells musty in the heat
and his heart beats wildly
desperate to spring free,
        to stir them from slumber.

Brother Andre Teaches Forgiveness

Brother Andre lies in a black oak box
in the midst of the choir
as we gather for Morning Prayer.
There he lies quite still
as we sit knowing everything.
No secrets, no past hidden.

The prayers begin, leading us
to the ways of mercy,
casting doubt on the finality of sin.
Andre, cold and stiff, lies at our feet,
His broken, diseased body smoothed
by the leveling power of death.

No one picks up a final stone.
No tongues cluck in judgment.
We know in this meeting
of life and death
the counting is over.
Past the veil Andre is free,
free from his damaged past,
free to fall forgiven
      into the arms of God.
And we envy him.

Lost Recipe

The soup's grown thin,
more water than substance,
the attention to flavor
replaced by disputes
over proper measure,
the shape of the pot
or height of flame.
All the while we hunger,
imagining
what it must have been
before we forgot
how to make a meal.

A New Age

These strangers who come
from a land much like our own
leave us puzzled.
Corseted in their prayers,
they drape a slim view of God
across their shoulders
and stand beneath the arches
judging passersby.
Their certainty annoys us
who've made the rounds
far less sure the rules
work so neatly.
We look at each other,
when they pass
with downcast eyes,
their soft hands adjusting
perfectly starched cuffs.

Think Again

Love your enemies?
Are you insane
Or simply playing the fool?
How many falls does it take
To prove the fist as final arbiter
For safety and peace of mind?

Jesus may have said it,
But his were different times.
Don't forget the temple,
His fit of righteous rage
Sending money changers fleeing
from his point emphatically made.

Advice about getting along
Shouldn't deny us recourse
When an eye has been punched,
Or a tooth knocked loose.
Keep a level head on these matters.
Religion's okay in times of doubt
But useless in a battle.

Searching For A Future

When the bursts of incense clear,
Will anyone be left?
Will there be enough for a choir,
For four-part harmony?
Or will it be all altos,
No tenors or bass?
How many strangers can we attract
With week-old doughnuts and
Coffee cooked
  to a deep,
        bitter,
                black?

All Souls Day

What we hope for
Is a bright lamp
Set high in a window
So the darkness,
Split like the Red Sea,
Will reveal a path
We can pass unafraid
And hear voices we know,
Our ears sharpened
By their absence.

Unbreakable Bond

We remember the dead.
Their faces line our dreams
or catch our eye
in the slant of light
at end of a summer's day.

We carry them like a talisman,
a carved piece of sorrow
worn smooth by its handling.
We have only memory for comfort,
its ministrations fragile and thin.

But our dead surround us
in this chaotic sea we still sail,
their faces our North Star,
our bond obscured
but never broken.

Communion of Saints

The ones called saints,
Iconed with shimmery halos,
Are hardly one of us.
We may find them heroic
But know we lack their zeal,
Their single-mindedness,
Their deep pious affections.

We are very ordinary,
Common vessels of clay
Often poorly formed
And only partially kilned.
We barely hold a basic measure
Much less some outpouring
Of divine magnitude.

Though they seem unblemished,
Rare jewels with no flaws,
those raised above the crowd
seldom wore seamless gowns.
Their halos, pious affectations,
Might illuminate their images in death
But in life went unseen.

It wasn't modesty or reluctance
For the saints knew their clayness,
Vessels with shapes askew and lopsided,
Some with deep cracks and pockmarks.
Not aimed toward hagiography,
They simply wondered how best to live
And then set full-hearted to the task.

Made in the USA
Charleston, SC
24 January 2012